BENJAMIN BRITTEN

AUDIO ACCESS INCLUDED
Recorded Accompaniments Online

MEDIUM/LOW VOICE

HENRY PURCELL
12 SELECTED SONGS
Realizations by Benjamin Britten

Music by Henry Purcell
The Figured Basses realized by Benjamin Britten
The Vocal Parts edited by Peter Pears

Edited by Richard Walters

Also Available:
THE PURCELL COLLECTION
Realizations by Benjamin Britten
High Voice (50 Songs)
Medium/Low Voice (45 Songs)
Boosey & Hawkes

To access companion recorded accompaniments online, visit:
www.halleonard.com/mylibrary

Enter Code
2175-2701-9698-4857

Boosey &Hawkes

DISTRIBUTED BY

HAL•LEONARD
CORPORATION
7777 W. BLUEMOUND RD. P.O. BOX 13819 MILWAUKEE, WI 53213

www.boosey.com
www.halleonard.com

CONTENTS

6   *About the Songs*

8   Fairest Isle
from *Seven Songs* (Orpheus Britannicus)

14   Hark the ech'ing air!
from *Five Songs* (Orpheus Britannicus)

11   How blest are shepherds
from *Five Songs* (Orpheus Britannicus)

22   I attempt from love's sickness to fly
from *Five Songs* (Orpheus Britannicus)

18   I'll sail upon the Dog-star
from *Seven Songs* (Orpheus Britannicus)

25   If music be the food of love (1st version)
from *Six Songs* (Orpheus Britannicus)

28   Man is for the woman made
from *Six Songs* (Orpheus Britannicus)

32   Music for a while
from *Seven Songs* (Orpheus Britannicus)

36   On the brow of Richmond Hill
from *Seven Songs* (Orpheus Britannicus)

44   There's not a swain of the plain
from *Six Songs* (Orpheus Britannicus)

39   Turn then thine eyes
from *Seven Songs* (Orpheus Britannicus)

46   We sing to him
from *Three Divine Hymns* (Harmonia Sacra)

HENRY PURCELL
1659—1695

Henry Purcell was the great English composer of the Baroque, internationally recognized as the most important British born composer prior to the twentieth century. He was the dominant musical presence of the London of his day, leaving a profound legacy of compositions. Little is known about much of his short life.

Purcell came from a family of musicians. His father and uncle were singers and lutenists in service to the royal court. His father likely died in 1664, but his probable uncle, Thomas Purcell, continued in various minor court music appointments through the 1670s. Young Henry's musical life began as a boy chorister, probably at the age of 9 or 10, in the Chapel Royal in London. This included a basic education, with a study of Latin, as well as music theory, and lessons on string and keyboard instruments. It is likely that he learned the lute or theorbo, the principal vocal accompaniment instruments of the day. Purcell's organ and keyboard studies were with Christopher Gibbons, a virtuoso and son of the composer Orlando Gibbons. A part-song from 1667 is attributed to Purcell, indicating that his talent for composition was apparent at a young age. Matthew Locke, composer and author of an influential treatise on continuo playing, may have been one of Purcell's early teachers. It is entirely possible that Purcell studied composition with John Blow in the 1670s. Blow (born in 1649) and Purcell sustained a close friendship, both professionally and personally, until Purcell's death. Scholars have theorized that the two composers borrowed ideas from one another regularly in their work.

After his voice broke, in his teen years Purcell was a music copyist, an organ tuner at Westminster Abbey, and an assistant in responsibility for the king's collections of musical instruments. He achieved his first important appointment as composer-in-ordinary for violins in 1677, and was named organist of Westminster Abbey in 1679, succeeding John Blow. Purcell's royal appointments continued to the end of his life, including being organist of the Chapel Royal, a singer in the Chapel's choir (he was a bass and countertenor), an organ maker, and keeper of the king's instruments.

There are records of Purcell compositions for royal occasions as early as 1680. He contributed music for official events until the funeral of Queen Mary in 1694. Purcell composed odes and welcome songs, instrumental pieces, choral anthems, keyboard music and songs for royal occasions. He wrote just as much music for other reasons as well, including an enormous output of songs and instrumental numbers as theatre music.

After the death of Charles II in 1685, there was a decline in royal patronage of music in the court of James II. The commercial music scene in London, especially in the theatre, began a rise to prominence. Purcell's musical career followed the same trends, with less music written for royal occasions and more theatre music being written from about 1690 on. Purcell's theatre music is overwhelmingly incidental in its function. London theatre during the restoration period greatly favored spoken drama, as opposed to opera on the continent, particularly in Italy. It would not be until the early decades of the eighteenth century that Italian opera would conquer the British capital. Despite the tastes of the era, Purcell was able to compose substantial scores for five semi-operas, or masques: *The Prophetess*, *King Arthur*, *The Fairy Queen*, *The Indian Queen*, *The Tempest*.

Purcell's only full-fledged opera, *Dido and Aeneas*, composed sometime during the 1680s, was not for a professional theatre, but for Josias Priest's School for Young Ladies, though it is not clear that the opera was ever performed during the composer's lifetime. Writing for that modest venue obviously did not prevent the appearance of Purcell's revolutionary concept of opera in English. The only other example of opera in the language during this period was his friend John Blow's *Venus and Adonis*. His semi-operas, *Dido and Aeneas*, his theatre songs and other works reveal a master composer of rare dramatic talents.

By the age of 20 or 21, Purcell had achieved a mature, individual style as an international composer that would continue to evolve over his short life, combining an English heritage with Italian music of his era, as well as incorporating French influences. He was a technical master in contrapuntal writing, especially evident in his canons and inventive compositions based on a ground bass, where melodies ingeniously spin out in phrase structures not aligned with the ground. His harmonies varied from primarily conservative in early works to chromaticism later on.

Purcell most remarkably advanced the setting of the English language in vocal music, with an individual, evolved style of marrying words and notes, inspired by the freedom of Italian composers in florid and expressive melismas.

Purcell died on 21 November 1695. An anecdote was perpetuated that he died from a cold caught when his wife locked him out of the house because of drunkenness. This is almost certainly untrue. There are indications that he enjoyed a particularly loving relationship with his wife, Frances, and their two children, Edward (who also became a musician) and Frances. Purcell was probably ill for some months before death. He died on the eve of the feast of St. Cecilia. The loss was a blow to the arts loving of London. He was buried at the foot of the organ in Westminster Abbey in a grandly solemn public service that included his own music. The inscription on his grave monument, attributed to John Dryden, states, "Here Lyes Henry Purcell Esq. Who left this life and is gone to that Blessed Place where only his Harmony can be exceeded." Composers, such as John Blow, and poets, such as John Dryden, wrote pieces in tribute to Purcell.

The following poem about him by "R.G." appeared in the posthumously published collection of Purcell works, *Orpheus Britannicus*:

So justly were his Soul and Body join'd,
You'd think his Form the Product of his Mind.
A Conqu'ring sweetness in his Vizage dwelt,
His eyes wou'd warm, his Wit like Lightning melt,
But those no more must now be seen, and that no more be felt.
Pride was the sole aversion of his Eye,
Himself as Humble as his Art was High.

ABOUT THE SONGS

The source for much of the information in this section:
Benjamin Britten: A Catalogue of the Published Works,
compiled and edited by Paul Banks,
published by The Britten-Pears Library for the Britten Estate Limited.

Songs from
ORPHEUS BRITANNICUS

Orpheus Britannicus (Latin for British Orpheus) was the original title of the Purcell song anthologies in multiple volumes, published posthumously, beginning in 1698. The subtitle of the publications: A Collection of all The Choicest Songs for One, Two and Three Voices.

from *Five Songs*
Realizations by Benjamin Britten composed 1939 to 1958. Published by Boosey & Hawkes
(high voice and piano), 1960.

Hark the ech'ing air!
Song by Purcell from *The Fairy Queen* (semi-opera), first performed at the Dorset Garden Theatre, London, 1692. Anonymous text, adapted from Shakespeare's *A Midsummer Night's Dream* (though there is no Shakespeare in the song texts). First known performance of the Britten realization: Peter Pears, tenor, Benjamin Britten, piano, 19 November 1939, Hotel Henry Perkins, Riverhead, New York. This realization is different from the complete 1967 version of *The Fairy Queen* edited and realized by Britten and Imogen Holst.

How blest are shepherds
Song by Purcell from *King Arthur* (semi-opera), first performed at the Dorset Garden Theatre, London, 1691. Text by John Dryden, apparently adapted to comment on current politics. It is a play with little resemblance to actual history, about legendary King Arthur, the magical accomplice Merlin, the capture of Arthur's betrothed Emmeline by the Saxons, ending with his defeat by the Saxon King Oswald. First known performance of the Britten realization: Peter Pears, tenor, Benjamin Britten, piano, 1 March 1958, Stuttgart, Germany.

I attempt from love's sickness to fly
Song by Purcell from *The Indian Queen* (semi-opera), first performed at the Drury Lane Theatre, London, 1695. Text by John Dryden and Robert Howard. Purcell's ultimately mortal illness prevented him from completing the score, work done by his composer brother Daniel. The plot concerns the impossible scenario of war between the Incas of Peru and the Aztecs of Mexico. Aztec queen Zempoalla sings of her unrequited love for the warrior Montezuma in this minuet *en rondeau*. First known performance of the Britten realization: Peter Pears, tenor, Benjamin Britten, piano, 26 April 1947, Teatro Comunale, Florence, X Maggio Musicale Fiorentino.

from *Seven Songs*
Realizations by Benjamin Britten composed 1943 to November 1945. Published by Boosey & Hawkes
(high voice and piano), 1947. Medium Voice transposed edition published by Boosey & Hawkes, 1948.

Fairest Isle
Song by Purcell from *King Arthur* (see "How blest are shepherds" for more information on *King Arthur*). "Fairest Isle," an ode to England, is sung by Venus near the end of the play. First known performance of the Britten realization: Peter Pears, tenor, or Margaret Ritchie, soprano (records are apparently unclear), Benjamin Britten, piano, 21 November 1945, Wigmore Hall, London.

I'll sail upon the Dog-star
Song by Purcell written as incidental theatre music for *A Fool's Preferment or The Three Dukes of Dunstable,* 1688. Text by Thomas D'Urfey. This mad rant is sung by Lyonel, a "well bred ingenious gentleman, who, being hindred of his Mistress, by the King, fell distracted," according to the *dramatis personae*. First known performance of the Britten realization: Peter Pears, tenor, Benjamin Britten, piano, 20 July 1943, BBC Home Service, England. Pears performed the song in April, 1943, with pianist Norman Franklin, but it is not known whether Britten's realization was used.

Music for a while
Song by Purcell with basso continuo, composed c. 1692. Text by John Dryden from *Oedipus*. Dryden had adapted *Oedipus* from Sophocles and Seneca in 1678, revived in the 1690s. The ground bass air "Music for a while" is from a scene calling up the spirit of King Laius to name the person who murdered him. The scene is of a blind seer, Tiresias, and two priests, one of whom launches into "Music for a while," addressed to the dead Laius. First known performance of the Britten realization: Peter Pears, tenor, or Joan Cross, soprano (records are apparently unclear), Benjamin Britten, piano, 17 November 1945, Philharmonic Hall, Liverpool, England. Britten's dedication: "For Joan Cross" (1900-1993).

On the brow of Richmond Hill
Song by Purcell with basso continuo, first published 1692. Text by Thomas D'Urfey. First known performance of the Britten realization: Peter Pears, tenor, Benjamin Britten, piano, 20 July 1943, BBC Home Service, England. Pears performed the song in April, 1943, with pianist Norman Franklin, but it is not known whether Britten's realization was used.

Turn then thine eyes
Song by Purcell with basso continuo, a solo version adapted from a duet from *The Fairy Queen*, date unknown. Anonymous text, adapted from Shakespeare's *A Midsummer Night's Dream* (though there is no Shakespeare in the song texts). First known performance of the Britten realization: Peter Pears, tenor, Benjamin Britten, piano, 13 March 1945, Salle de l'Ancien Conservatoire, Paris.

from *Six Songs*
Realizations by Benjamin Britten composed 1943 to November 1945. Published by Boosey & Hawkes (high voice and piano), 1947. Medium Voice transposed edition published by Boosey & Hawkes, 1948.

If music be the food of love (1st version)
Song by Purcell with basso continuo, first published c. 1694. Text by Henry Heveningham. The song was first published in a magazine published by Peter Anthony Motteux, a Huguenot from Rouen, *The Gentleman's Journal: or The Monthly Miscellany*. The opening line is by Shakespeare, the rest by Heveningham. Purcell's second version, published in 1695, is more ambitious vocally, in an Italian style. First known performance of the Britten realization: Peter Pears, tenor, Benjamin Britten, piano, 23 November 1945, National Gallery, London.

Man is for the woman made
Song by Purcell written as incidental theatre music for *The Mock Marriage*, 1695. Text by Peter Anthony Motteux. First known performance of the Britten realization: Peter Pears, tenor, or Margaret Ritchie, soprano (records are apparently unclear), Benjamin Britten, piano, 21 November 1945, Wigmore Hall, London.

There's not a swain of the plain
Song by Purcell with basso continuo, interpolated into the stage production *Rule a Wife and Have a Wife*, 1693. Text by Anthony Henly. First known performance of the Britten realization: Peter Pears, tenor, Benjamin Britten, piano, 19 July 1943, Mayflower Barn, Jordans, Buckinghamshire, England.

Song from
HARMONIA SACRA

The original title of Henry Playford's publication of Purcell's material was *Harmonia Sacra, or Divine Hymns and Dialogues*, published in two editions, 1688 and 1693.

from *Three Divine Hymns*
Realizations by Benjamin Britten composed 1944-45. Published by Boosey & Hawkes (high voice and piano), 1947. Medium Voice transposed edition published by Boosey & Hawkes, 1948. Britten's dedication: "To Imogen Holst" (1907-1984).

We sing to him
Song by Purcell for soprano, soprano and bass with basso continuo, first published 1688. Text by Nathaniel Ingelo. First known performance of the Britten realization: Peter Pears, tenor, Benjamin Britten, piano, 11 January 1946, Kleine Zaal, Concertgebouw, Amsterdam.

Fairest Isle

original key: B♭ Major

JOHN DRYDEN

HENRY PURCELL
realized by
BENJAMIN BRITTEN

In accompaniment recording, the first chord is played before the entrance so that the singer may get the pitch.

How blest are shepherds

from *King Arthur*

original key: G Major

JOHN DRYDEN

HENRY PURCELL
realized by
BENJAMIN BRITTEN

low - ly sheds all the __ storm pass - es, __ And when we die 'tis in
emp - ty, and when youth is __ end - ed, __ All men will praise you but

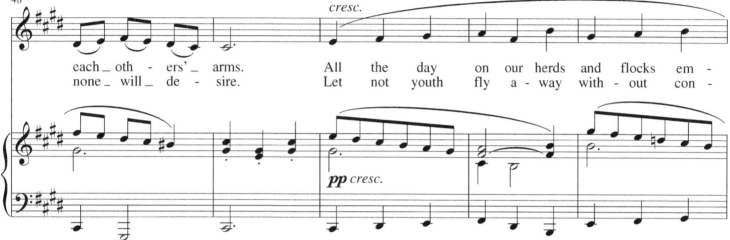

cresc.

each __ oth - ers' __ arms. All the day on our herds and flocks em -
none __ will __ de - sire. Let not youth fly a - way with - out con -

pp cresc.

p

ploy - ing, All the night on our flutes and in en - joy - ing.
tent - ing, Age will come time e - nough for your re - pent - ing.

p

f

pp

Hark the ech'ing air!

original key: B♭ Major

ANONYMOUS

HENRY PURCELL
realized by
BENJAMIN BRITTEN

sings. And all _____ a -

round, and all _____ a - round, pleased _____

Cu - pids clap _ their wings, clap, clap, clap, clap _ their wings, pleased _

_____ Cu - pids clap their _ wings, and all _____ a -

round, and all_____ a - round, pleased _____

lightly

Cu - pids clap, _ clap, clap, _ clap, clap their _ wings, clap their

wings, clap their wings, clap their wings, pleased _____

Cu - pids clap their wings. And all_____ a - wings.

I'll sail upon the Dog-star

original key: B♭ Major

THOMAS D'URFEY

HENRY PURCELL
realized by
BENJAMIN BRITTEN

moon till it be noon, I'll chase _____ the _ moon till it be

noon but I'll make, I'll make her _ leave _ her horn - ing.

I'll climb the frost - y moun - tain, I'll climb the frost - y

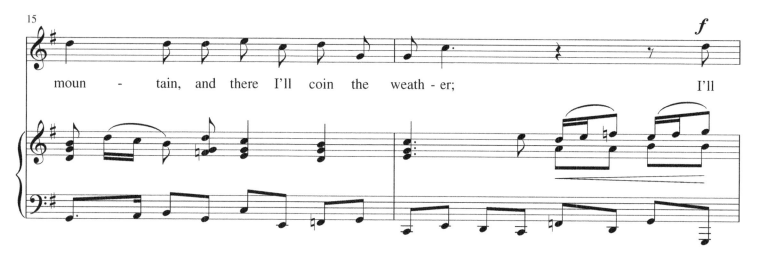

moun - tain, and there I'll coin the weath - er; I'll

tear _____ the _ rain - bow from the sky, I'll tear _____ the _

rain - bow from _ the _ sky and tie, _____ and _ tie _ both _

ends to - geth - er. The

stars pluck from their orbs too, the stars pluck from their orbs too, and

crowd them in my budg - et; and

wheth - er I'm a __ roam - - - - - ing boy,

pesante

marc.

a roam - - - ing boy, let all, _____

__ let __ all __ the __ Na - tion judge it.

ff con forza

I attempt from love's sickness to fly

original key: A Major

JOHN DRYDEN
and ROBERT HOWARD

HENRY PURCELL
realized by
BENJAMIN BRITTEN

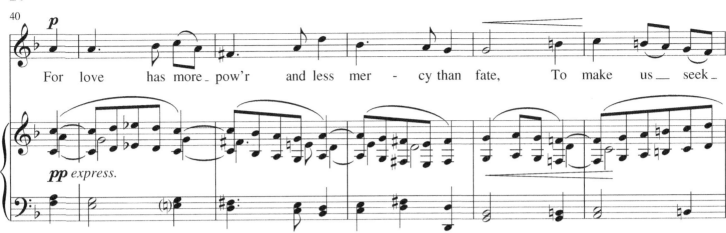

For love has more pow'r and less mer - cy than fate, To make us seek

ru - in, to make us seek ru - in and love those that hate. I at-

tempt from love's sick - ness to fly _____ in vain, Since

I am my - self my own fe - ver, since I am my - self my own fe - ver and pain.

If music be the food of love

(1st Version)

original key: G minor

HENRY HEVENINGHAM

HENRY PURCELL
realized by
BENJAMIN BRITTEN

In accompaniment recording, the first chord is played before the entrance so that the singer may get the pitch.

Man is for the woman made

Roundelay

original key: C Major

PETER ANTHONY MOTTEUX

HENRY PURCELL
realized by
BENJAMIN BRITTEN

In accompaniment recording, the first chord is played before the entrance so that the singer may get the pitch.

man is for the wom - an made and the wom - an for the

man. Be she wi - dow be she maid, Be she

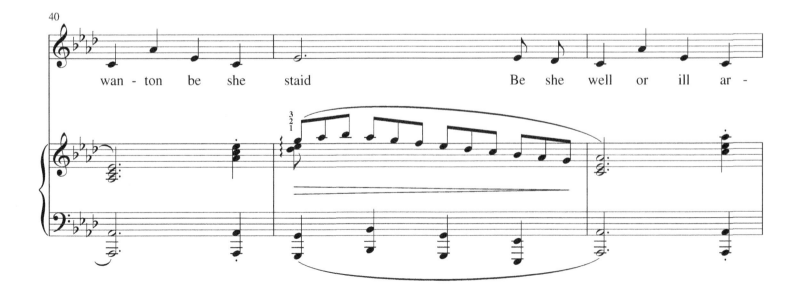

wan - ton be she staid Be she well or ill ar -

ray'd, Prin - cess or har - ri - dan, So

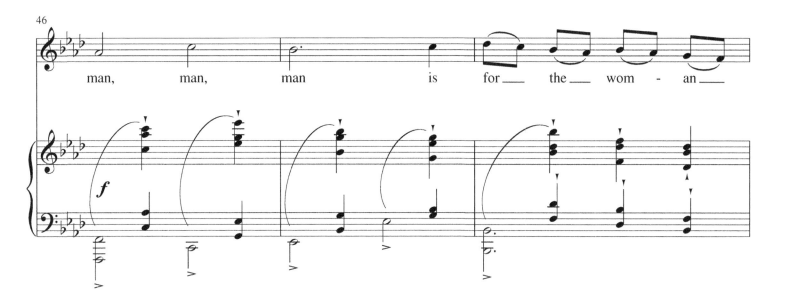

man, man, man is for__ the__ wom - an__

made and the wom - an for__ the man_____

For Joan Cross

Music for a while

original key: a perfect 4th higher

JOHN DRYDEN

HENRY PURCELL
realized by
BENJAMIN BRITTEN

Andante con moto

Mu - sic, mu - sic for a while, Shall all your cares be-

guile; Shall all, all, all, Shall all, all, all, Shall all your cares be -

On the brow of Richmond Hill

original key: B♭ Major

THOMAS D'URFEY

HENRY PURCELL
realized by
BENJAMIN BRITTEN

In accompaniment recording, the first chord is played before the entrance so that the singer may get the pitch.

Thames doth glide and state - ly courts are ed - i - fied.

Mead - ows deck'd in sum - mer's pride, with ver - dant beau - ties

crowned. Love - ly Cyn - thia pas - sing by, with

bright - er glo - ries blest my eye, Ah! then in

vain in vain said I, the fields and

poco a poco cresc.

flowers do shine; Na - ture in this charm - ing place, cre -

at - ed pleas - ure in ex - cess, But all are poor to

rall. al fine

Cyn - thia's face, whose fea - tures are di - vine.

Turn then thine eyes

original key: A minor

ANONYMOUS

HENRY PURCELL
realized by
BENJAMIN BRITTEN

⊕ In the "Orpheus Britannicus" this is a duet; but Purcell also did a solo-voice version.

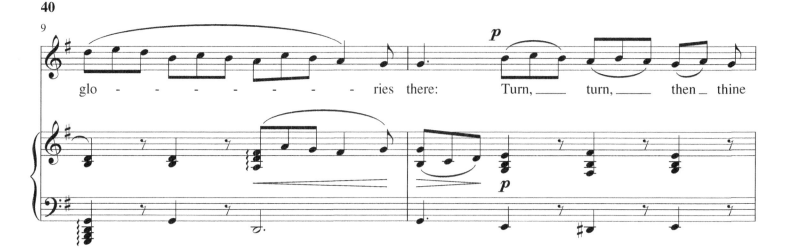

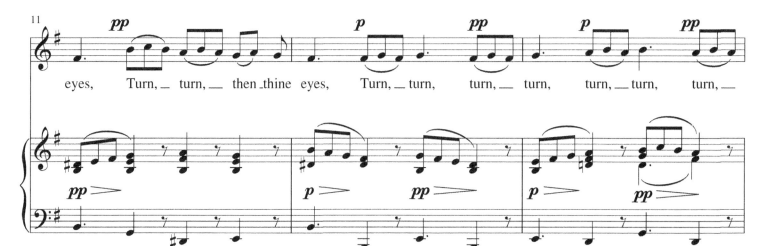

There's not a swain of the plain

original key: E minor

ANTHONY HENLY

HENRY PURCELL
realized by
BENJAMIN BRITTEN

In accompaniment recording, the first chord is played before the entrance so that the singer may get the pitch.

When I cry, must I die? You＿ make＿ no re-ply, But look shy And＿ with a

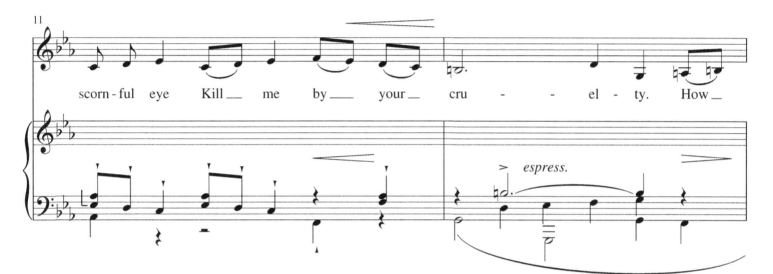

scorn-ful eye Kill＿ me by＿ your＿ cru - - el - ty. How＿

can you be, can you be, can you be, can you be, can you be, can you be,

can you be, Can you, can you, can you be so hard to me?

We sing to him

original key: a perfect 4th higher

NATHANIEL INGELO

HENRY PURCELL
realized by
BENJAMIN BRITTEN

In accompaniment recording, the first note is played before the entrance so that the singer may get the pitch.